MAKE YOUR OWN

WOODEN FLUTE

MAKE YOUR OWN WOODEN FLUTE

Steve Schmeck

ManyTracks

www.ManyTracks.com

Table of Contents

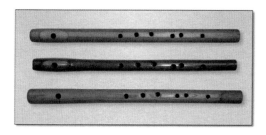

Introduction

In all my years working with wood I've found that some of the most satisfying projects have been the making of musical instruments. I have built everything from simple board zithers to lap and hammered dulcimers to wooden flutes. Back in our art fair days the flutes were one of the most popular things we sold. Some of the flutes were pretty basic; a hardwood tube with holes drilled in strategic locations. On some I carved a raised lip plate and others I carved the closed end; bird, cat, human face, among other designs.

I really did enjoy both making the flutes and (there seems to be a pattern here) making the tools and jigs to make them more efficiently and of better quality. The two tools I made that were most helpful were a hand-powered boring machine and my trusty treadle lathe. I have already written about the lathe in "Make Your Own Treadle Lathe" which is available as an eBook at most on-line book retailers and as a paperback at Amazon and Createspace. Now I'd like to share with you my flute-making experiences: the materials, tools, jigs and the building process.

Just so we are on the same page, these flutes are 'simple flutes'. They are cross-blown, tubular wind instruments with the holes covered by your fingers - as opposed to fancy levers and pads. Also, the instruments I'm describing here are what I call 'wander in the woods' flutes; designed to be played solo or possibly with other folk instruments, not in an orchestral setting.

I hope that you enjoy making and playing your new wooden flute!

1 – Tools

- Hand brace*

- Ships auger at least 14" long**

- 1/2" dowel for sanding the bore

- Treadle lathe & cutting tools (you *could* use a regular, powered wood lathe)

- Sandpaper, 100/150/220/320 grits

- 15" ruler or yard stick

- Hand drill with 5/16", 9/32" and 1/4" drill bits (see text)

- 1/4" rat tail rasp

- Workbench or sturdy table & a couple of clamps

- Hatchet and/or draw-knife

- Spokeshave

* Some older braces have only two jaw pieces so you may need to grind a couple of flats on the end of the auger bit to get the brace to hold it well.

** An on-line search for "11/16 ship auger" found them priced from $15 - $42; Amazon $20, Home Depot $20. If sharpened well I suspect that any of them would do the job we're asking of it.

2 – The Process - Summary

Your tool inventory will to some extent determine the actual details of the flute making process. I'll describe a more or less handmade method and mention the specialized tools as we come to them.

Here are the basic steps:

• Select appropriate stock and cut it to a workable size

• Drill the long hole down most of the length of the blank

• Locate the center of the bore on the 'closed' end of the blank

• Rough trim the blank down close to the bore, making it a rough tube

• Turn the tube down on the lathe until the tube sidewalls are about 1/8" thick

• Mark the locations of the mouth-hole and six finger holes

• Drill the holes

• Clean up the inside of the bore

• Play each note and adjust its pitch using a piano or electronic tuner

• Fine-sand the outside of the flute and apply oil finish. Whew, you're done!

3 – Stock Selection

You will need a wood blank about 2" x 2" x 17" long. This stock could be smaller, say 1-1/2" x 1-1/2" but the smaller the blank is the better your aim has to be when boring it. I <u>have</u> drilled right out of the side; usually caused by a combination of the grain not being straight or parallel with the sides of the blank. Other contributing factors were: a slight drill bit misalignment and/or operator over-optimism.

Nearly all of the flutes I've made have been from black cherry though I have made a few from maple, walnut and locust. The ideal stock would be knot-free, straight grained hardwood. I've chosen cherry for a couple of reasons. Of the fruit woods available here it has the most predictable grain and is relative easy to bore from the end. Apple or pear would make fine flutes but my experience has been that they are difficult to end-bore with hand tools. The other woods I've used showed no acoustic advantages over cherry and were either harder to work or unstable (locust).

Green wood from recently cut trees is easiest to bore but one must be patient enough to let the tube dry well before going on to the turning and following steps. Green tubes also tend to create slightly oval bores. I have not found this to be a problem acoustically.

Of course wood selection is one of the places where you are free to experiment. As long as you don't have to pay much for the small piece of stock, what do you have to lose? My advice, based upon personal experience, is to stay away from softer woods like pine, poplar and basswood as they tend to tear when bored.

4 – Boring the Blank:

The blank used in this book

This is one area where tool selection can really make a difference. I have been using a 11/16" ships auger. These bits occasionally show up in yard sales but can be purchased new (& sharp) for less than $30 online.

Use masking tape to mark the length you want to bore; 14 1/8" from the front edge of the bit's cutter.

I have ground flats onto the shaft of one of these long bits and bored flute blanks using a standard hand brace. It is easier to get the bit aimed straight down the blank if you use a centering jig or have a helper with a good eye to guide you. Once the bit is in a couple of inches you won't be able to change its direction so the initial alignment is critical to avoid coming out the side of the blank.

For working alone I came up with several bore alignment jigs that worked well when using dimensioned lumber or a reasonably squared up blank. First, the *fancy* jig.

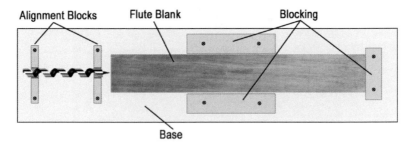

Bore alignment jig

I began with a 1" x 8" board about 28" long and drew a line lengthwise down its center to help align both the alignment blocks and the blank. Then I drilled 11/16" holes in two 1" x 3" hardwood scraps...

Alignment Blocks

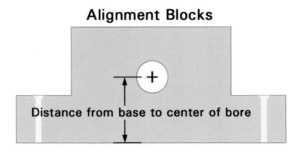

and screwed them into position about 8" apart, aligning the center lines of the guide blocks with the centerline on the base. Putting a long dowel temporarily in the blocks made the alignment easier. The blocking for the sides and far end of the blank were made from 2" x 2" pine drilled for deck or drywall screws.

The flute blank is centered on the base and the blocking screwed down to hold the blank in place. If the blank seems too loose for comfort you can tap a thin wedge or two between the side blocking and the flute blank. Once you have bored in as far as you can without the brace running into the jig you can remove the blocking and put the blank in a vise or clamp it to a bench to finish the job.

Now, the *not-so-fancy* jig. While in a less ambitious mode and unable to locate the above jig, I got by with just one alignment block clamped near the end of my work bench. The flute-blank was then clamped with a large adjustable bar clamp to the bench. Alignment is fairly critical, both horizontal and vertical, but pretty easy to do by eye.

Ready to bore using a simple alignment jig

Use your ship auger and a hand brace to bore into the end of the flute blank 4 or 5 inches. The self-feeding tip of the bit should keep the cutting action going but sometimes, especially with dryer, harder woods, it can lose its grip. If that happens you will need to clear the chips by pulling the bit out and then re-insert it, pressing firmly forward while turning the brace to get the tip grabbing again. In fact, even if the boring process is going well it doesn't hurt to back the bit out a few turns to disengage the tip and gently withdraw the bit to clear the chips. The long spiral edges of a new bit are very sharp and the bits themselves are somewhat flexible. If the chips build up in the bore they can force the bit sideways and cause the sharp sides of the bit to enlarge the bore as well as making it really hard to get the bit out.

Stop boring when you reach the depth marking tape. It is so much fun and feels cool (there is a certain, crunchy sound and feel when hand-boring end grain in hardwood) it's easy to forget that you don't want to go right out the end of the blank. I truth I've done that and all was not lost. I just turned a plug from a contrasting color wood and glued it in place with waterproof glue.

Boring Machine

Since I was making quite a few flutes back in the '80's I put together this boring machine.

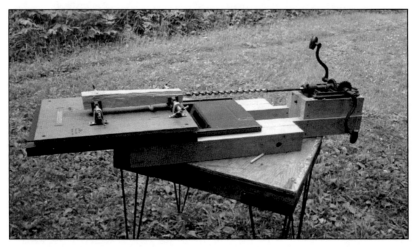

Steve's boring machine

It was made up from an old log cabin-maker's boring tool, a copy machine sliding table and Jorgensen pipe clamps. Strange? Ugly? Well, it worked great and bored lots of flute blanks! The primary advantage of the boring machine over the boring jig was that I could quickly clamp a blank onto the deck, slide it firmly into the end of the drill bit's self-feeding screw tip, and crank away. There is a pin that stops the sliding table at exactly the depth I wanted. It would take five minutes in all to bore a blank.

Here are a couple of photos of the ol' boring machine in action:

Blank aligned and ready to be bored

Setting the bit

5 – Finding the Center

Finding the center of the bore in the blind end of the blank, a rather tricky step, was greatly simplified by this center-finder gizmo.

Center finders

My first center-finder was made from a scrap piece of angle iron and some threaded rod. It is nice and sturdy, which is good, but I also made up a wooden version with a couple of dowels and scraps as shown on the right.

The shorter of the two dowels was wrapped with masking tape at the top and near the bottom to be a reasonably snug fit inside the bore. In use, the base is clamped in a vise or to the bench, the bored blank is carefully lowered onto the shorter post and the marking arm is installed on the taller post. With a soft-lead pencil I draw a line next to the 'pointer' as I swing the marking arm across the top of the blank. Then rotate the blank 90 degrees and do it again. I repeat this twice more and unless the pointer was miraculously centered over the exact center of the shorter post, I end up with something like a '#' (see photo below). If all has gone well, and you have been careful to not push either post out of position, the center of the # will be the center of the bore.

Center finder in use

During setup that little pointer (drywall screw) is aligned right over the center of the shorter dowel. I have to admit that the all metal version is easier to use because it is less likely to be distorted during use, but I have used both center finders with good success.

6 – Roughing the Blank

At this point you should have an over-sized piece with the bored hole in one end and the bore center marked on the other. In this next step we'll mark the shape of the tube hidden within the blank, first on the ends and then on the sides. Using these lines as guides you can then use a hatchet, draw-knife or whatever tools you have and are most comfortable with to reduce the blank to a rough cylindrical shape.

Draw a 1-1/2" circle on each end of the blank centered around the hole on the open end and around the center mark on the other. Next, draw lines on either side of the circles, perpendicular to the faces of the blank and carry the ends of those lines a bit over onto the faces. Finally, connect the marks down the faces. If you started with a more or less square blank this step will be easier since you will have four faces to mark. By the way, I've used a Sharpie® marker - you want to be able to see all these lines well. The photos show all this better than I can say it:

Marking the blank for reduction

I first chopped some of the bigger areas off with a small hatchet then moved to the shaving horse (a sturdy vise would work fine) and systematically removed wood with a draw-knife to get down to a four-sided shape, hopefully with the tube safely centered within it. You might need to re-mark the face lines as you go. In the photo below you can see the tube-reducing sequence.

Shaping the tube

Tube Roughing Jig

The process described above is how I rough out individual flute blanks but I thought I'd share with you one more special tool I created to expedite the roughing process when making a batch of flutes. I use this tool on my trusty old '50's ShopSmith® set up as a table saw. It would probably work as well on a bandsaw that has a fence.

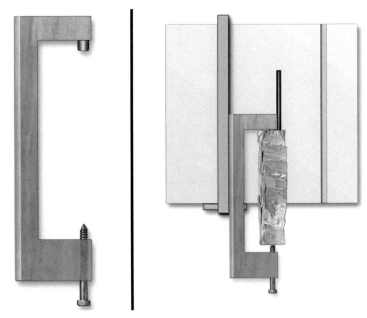

The way this works is...

- Use a center punch to make a good hole on the center of the closed end of the blank

- Slide the bored hole of the rough blank onto the 11/16" stub at the top

- Turn the pointed screw at the bottom into the closed end center until it is very secure

- Set the tool/blank on the saw table, beveled edge against the fence, and adjust the fence so the blade lines up just outside the far side of the circle you drew on the open end of the blank.

- Make your first cut with the flattest, most stable, side of the blank against the table. Watch for pinching or kickback as the blank may tip a bit during the cut. If it does, you didn't have the screw tight enough or your feed rate is too fast.

- Rotate the blank so the just-cut face is down on the table and double-check and adjust the fence so the blade is aimed at the outside edge of that circle on the end.

- Make three more cuts and maybe re-do the first-cut side to end up with a square tube.

- Now rotate the square tube so the corners are aligned vertically, tighten it up and saw off each of the corners. When you're done you will have a nice octagonal tube.

The bevel on the left edge of the jig allows you to safely tilt the blank away from the blade when each cut is completed.

Using this tool I can rough out a blank in less than 10 minutes, even with all the setup time. Of course, if you will be making just a few flutes it is faster to do the job by hand – and you won't have yet another 'special' tool to store and lose. Disclaimer: I have used this tool successfully for many years with no safety-related problems but admit to being extremely cautious using the table saw. If you do make a tool like this please go slow and easy and watch where your fingers are. That first cut, with an uneven shape against the table may tilt and pinch as the cut progresses.

Now, back to the handmade methods!

7 – Marking the location of the lip plate (optional)

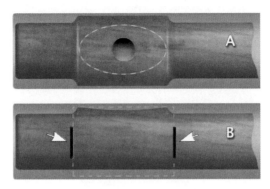

Locating the lip plate

As I mentioned above, some of my flutes have been simple, straight tube instruments but I have made some with carved ends and raised lip plates. If you plan on making a straight-tube flute you can skip on ahead to the next section.

If you wish to add a decorative carving or raised lip plate to your flute you will need to plan ahead and leave a thicker area on the tube for these additions. For a carved end you will just leave a thicker area at the end - enough for whatever you wish to carve.

For a raised lip plate you will need to do a little measuring. On an 'A' flute with a bore length of 14-1/8" the mouth-hole will be about 13-1/8" from the open end. This measurement allows for a bit (1/16") of finishing of the open end of the flute. A raised area about 2" long should work. Measure and make marks 12-1/8" and 14-1/8" from the open end of the blank. I use a #2 pencil rather than a felt marker for this since a marker may bleed deeply into the wood and show in the finished flute.

When turning, leave the area between the marks about 1/8" higher than the body of the flute. Later, when finishing the flute, you will carve away everything but the lip plate leaving the back and sides as a continuation of the body of the flute.

8 – Turning the tube

Begin the tube turning process by using the lathe to create a plug to insert into the tube-blank to give your tail center something to hold onto. On the closed end mark the usual X to match your drive center.

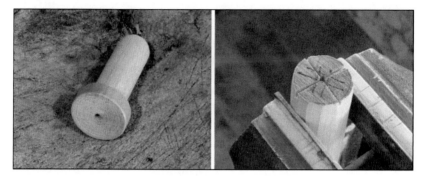

Tube centering plug

I use just three or four lathe tools for this project: roughing gouge, small skew, parting tool and if I'm creating a raised lip plate, a small round gouge.

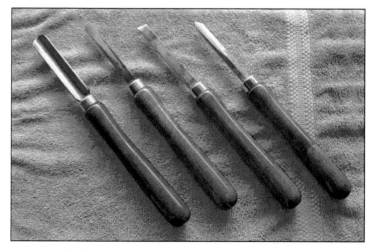

Lathe tools used when turning a flute tube

If you have read my Make Your Own Treadle Lathe book you may remember that I made provisions for mounting a long, straight tool rest to the lathe's uprights. Below you can see the tube mounted on my lathe and the long tool rest fastened in place with a pair wing nuts.

Tube ready to be turned on the treadle lathe

The actual lathe work on the flute project is pretty straight-forward. I use the roughing gouge to take off the high spots, switching to the skew once the tube is a nice cylinder. There are a couple of things that seem to be unique to turning a hollow tube, not the least, of course, is not breaking through the tube.

Just because we know where the bore is at both ends doesn't mean that we know for sure where it is along the whole length. This is because the ship auger, unlike a gun drill, can flex a bit and create a somewhat curved bore. We have tried to reduce the likelihood of this happening by selecting straight-grained stock but more than once I have been surprised, either by cutting right into the bore or noticing a thin spot. With this in mind, I stop periodically and pinch the tube around the middle to see if I can detect any softness or flexing. If I do notice some flexing I remove the tube from the lathe, take out the plug and hold the suspected thin area toward a bright light, sighting down the inside of the tube. If I detect any light I know that it is time to stop turning. If the tube is too big to make a comfortable feeling flute it's into the stove and back to step one. On the other hand, if the tube is only slightly thinned and is small enough to look and play OK, I mark the <u>thick</u> side lightly with a pencil and plan on drilling the mouth and finger holes on that side.

Checking tube diameter

The other thing you will probably notice is that the tube flexes quite a bit when cutting near the middle. Closer to the ends all is well but as the tube side walls get thinner I seem to experience more chatter. One solution is to support the tube with your 'other' hand (gloved). In any event, as the tube thins you will want to use lighter cuts, especially in the center area, to head off a potentially disastrous catch.

Once the tube is turned down to about 1" you might want to consider switching to sanding on the lathe. On the flute in the photos I put a quarter sheet of 60-grit on a flat sanding block to flatten off the contour and then worked my way through 100, 150 and 220-grit paper. Lots of dust in your face with this process so be sure to use a good dust mask or respirator with clean particle filters. I've been using a *Dust-be-gone®* washable dust mask and it has been working well for me.

Rough-sanding the tube to final shape

Sanding on the lathe with coarse sandpaper on a block removes wood pretty quickly. As above, you will want to periodically check that the tube walls are fairly symmetrical, that is, there are no thin spots. Unless you have a custom thickness gauge (maybe a future project?) you can hold the tube under a bright, direct light, rotate the tube looking for some light to show through. If you don't see a glowing area you can assume that the bore is pretty much centered in the tube. If you do notice a bit of a glow but the tube still seems to be strong in that area, make a pencil mark on the <u>other</u>, thicker side of the tube; you will drill the holes on that side.

9 – Carving the Lip Plate

If you have elected to make your flute without a raised lip plate you can skip on ahead to the next section on drilling the mouth and finger holes.

As I mentioned earlier, some of my flutes have a raised lip plate. This makes them look a little cooler and might, according to some sources, make the flute easier to play. I have not found any difference in playability but did find that when I had several instruments on display, the ones with lip plates usually sold first. You can see the profiles I've been using:

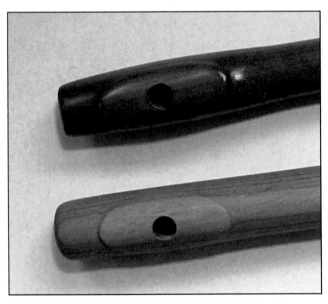

Some lip plate shape options

Begin by sanding the open end of your flute tube square (perpendicular to the length) so you will have a good reference point to start from. Measure 33.1 cm from the open end (on the thick side if you have one). Yes, I'm going metric all of a sudden. It seems easier for me to measure and mark centimeters and millimeters than to work with 64ths of an inch. I usually plan on the holes being on the flat, wider grain side if there is a choice. This seems to make it less likely that the drill bit will wander and makes shaping the holes easier, too.

Over the years I have used several different shapes for the lip plates. I usually make a thin cardboard or plastic template, position it over the mouth-hole and trace the shape. Here are some of my templates.

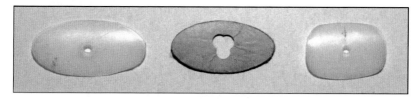

Lip plate templates

It is also OK to just use a soft lead pencil to draw an oval lip plate shape to your liking centered on the mouth-hole mark. Then, as they say in all those carving books, carve away everything outside that oval that doesn't look like a flute lip plate. I begin by carefully using a spoke shave on the back and sides of the tube. Then I use a very sharp detail knife to outline the lip plate and carve it down to blend in with the turned tube.

Various flute-end treatments
Carved cat, inlayed colored floss, flared end

10 – Marking & Boring the Mouth and Finger Holes

Layout tools

Tube length and mouth-hole placement determines the overall pitch of the instrument while finger hole placement determines the pitch of the individual notes. Some refined simple flutes are capable of playing two octaves but in the hands of a relatively inexperienced or beginning player I have found that my flutes usually do best in their native octave. In other words, for these flutes with a 11/16" bore and 14" bore length, you should be able to play one full octave in the key of 'A'. An experienced flautist will probably be able to get well up into the second octave.

After reading a few books on flute and recorder construction I eventually came up with a finger hole spacing and sizing pattern that is pretty accurate and yields an easily playable flute. There are many theories about what makes for a good sounding, pitch-correct instrument and I don't claim to be an expert on the subject. The 'wander-in-the-woods' (perhaps not super-accurate pitch) nature of my flutes is what I was after from the beginning, as opposed to an orchestral-sounding instrument.

Below are the hole center measurements for your flute. I've used a metric scale because I have found it easier to communicate centimeters vs. 64ths of an inch. Do your best in marking and then drilling the holes. We'll be fine-tuning the flute later but getting the holes drilled accurately will make the tuning process a lot easier.

Marking hole locations with template

Before marking these hole centers assure that the open end of your flute tube is square (perpendicular to the length). Later you can fine-tune the flute by sanding more off the end if necessary and then rounding the edges for comfort and appearance.

Mouth-hole center: 33.1cm from finished open end of the tube

Finger holes are all measured from the center of the mouth-hole.

    #1: 12.25 cm

    #2: 15.2 cm

    #3: 17.9 cm

    #4: 21.4 cm

    #5: 23.05 cm

    #6: 27.0 cm

Since I can't easily loan you my little acrylic template, I've created a printable version that can be downloaded, printed out and taped into position to mark your tube. You can just use the measurements above but I think that the template may give you better results. The trick will be to be sure that the printed and assembled template doesn't get resized in the printing process. The template is in PDF format and can be downloaded here: http://www.manytracks.com/flutes/hole-template-printable.pdf I have included instructions on how to assemble (it is too long for letter-sized paper) and use the template.

Once you have marked and double-checked the spacing it's time to drill the holes. Some of these holes will be enlarged later. Here are the drill bit sizes that I use:

    ¤ Mouth-hole and holes #1, #2 & #3: 5/16"

    ¤ Holes #4 & #5: 9/32"

    ¤ Hole #6: 1/4"

How not to drill the finger-holes

I have a really nice set of super sharp brad point bits I bought for myself in a time of perceived affluence. I tried to drill flute holes with one of these bits in a hand drill with disastrous results:

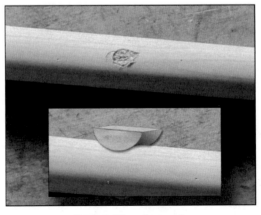

Bad drilling & repair

In the photo on the previous page you can see the mess I created because the spurs of the brad-point bit snagged on the crest of the curve of the tube. I repaired the damage by turning a two-step dowel about 6" long with one half of the dowel turned about 1/32" smaller than the other. I then wrapped a piece of #150 sandpaper around the smaller portion and created a dished area over the damaged spot. The smaller part of the dowel compensated for the thickness of the sandpaper so the larger end of the dowel was a nice fit in the recess. A segment of the thicker end of the dowel was glued into the recess with epoxy and once cured was shaved down and finished with the rest of the flute. Lesson learned: Either use regular drill bits that shouldn't take off like the brad-points or, as I did on this flute, use the best bits you have in a drill press. That brings us to another point: how do you safely hold the tube for operations like drilling the mouth and finger holes?

Holding the flute tube

Care must be taken in holding the tube for drilling. It would be very easy to crush the tube if ruthlessly clamped in a vise, even if carefully clamped in a vise and then pressed upon with a drill bit. What I have come up with for this step is a V-block lined with leather. It is clamped to my bench for hand work or to the drill press table.

V-block flute tube holder

I use it with the 'hinged' hold-down – also V'd and lined with leather, or open which seems to work better on the dill press.

When the holes have all been drilled it's time to sand the inside of the bore. The quality of sound of a flute is greatly influenced by the smoothness of the bore. The best tool I have come up with for this is a 16" long 5/8" dowel with a slit in the end to accept various grits of sandpaper. Here is what it looks like:

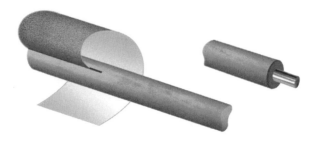

I drilled a ¼" hole in the end and glued in a cut-off ¼" bolt using epoxy. I use this tool by hand at first, until the worst of the splinters from drilling are removed, then chuck the shaft in a variable-speed drill for the rest of the bore cleanup.

It would be tempting to clamp the flute in a vise or the v-block and go at it with the dowel mounted in a hand drill. The problem (from experience) is that when, not if, the sandpaper/dowel jams in the tube it will want to wrench the flute out of the vise. The best I have done is to chuck the dowel in my variable speed electric hand drill, hold the tube in my left hand and gently work the spinning dowel up and down the bore. When the dowel jams I just release my grip a little and all is well.

Make the tube as smooth on the inside as you reasonably can, going through the sandpaper from 100 to 320, without thinning it too much.

11 – Tuning the flute

Let's clean up and shape the mouth (blow) hole next. For a child with small lips and not a lot of wind the 5/16" mouth-hole would be fine. For a larger child or adult I like to enlarge the mouth-hole to nearly 3/8". It seems to take a bit more wind but the sound is likely to be fuller. I use a rat-tail file to carefully enlarge the hole. A slight oval shape will also work OK.

Mouth-hole Sizes & Shapes

Once you have the mouth-hole sized and shaped as you'd like it, smooth the inside vertical surfaces of the hole with 220 sandpaper wrapped around a 1/4" or 5/16" dowel. Keep the back and sides of the hole vertical. The far side, the one away from you if you hold the flute with the open end to your right, can be slightly undercut as long as you maintain the shape. The edges should be left pretty sharp at this point.

You should be able to blow across the mouth-hole now and create a flute-sound. Unless you have experience playing a flute you will probably make some vaguely musical sound with a lot of air sounds. Try placing your lip just below the mouth-hole and blow a gentle, thin stream of air across the hole like you might if doing the old blowing-over-a-pop-bottle thing. While doing that roll the flute slightly away or toward you and you should find the 'sweet spot' where the best tone is produced. Being able to find this spot whenever you pick up the flute is a big part of learning to play it. The reason we're dealing with this sound business now is that, not surprisingly, you need to be able to make a fairly steady musical sound to tune the flute.

With all of the finger holes covered the flute should make its native pitch, an 'A' note, or fairly close to it. If you have a pitch pipe or better yet a chromatic electronic tuner, you should be able to confirm the native pitch. At this point you will begin to realize that there is more to creating a nice, clear, on-pitch tone with a cross-blown flute. Things like lip position, breath intensity and direction of the blown air, even the humidity inside the flute affect the sound. Every flute player has to deal with these variables on every note blown. It constantly amazes me that the human mind/body can learn to compensate for all these variables - with enough practice, of course.

Back to tuning! If the fundamental, native pitch (all holes well covered) is flat (lower than A) then shorten the tube a bit by sanding the open end. Go slow, sanding off perhaps 1/64" at a time, until you can consistently get a nice clear A note. Now, work your way up the scale, removing one finger at a time to see how close to true pitch the rest of the notes are. Here are the notes you are shooting for:

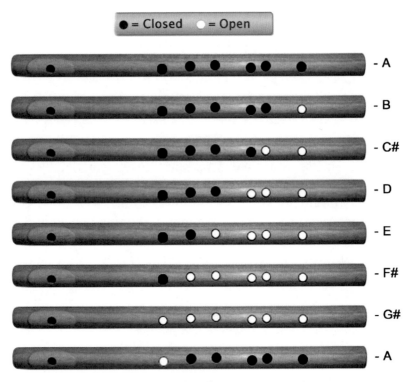

(Blown just a bit thinner & harder)

There are a couple of ways to raise the pitch of a note:

1- Enlarge the hole; preferably in an oval shape in line with the direction your finger will cover the hole. Be aware that it is possible to enlarge the hole beyond the point where the player's fingers can cover the hole easily.

2 - Undercut the hole in the direction of the mouth-hole. I use a small dowel wrapped with fine sandpaper for this.

Either method will work. I tend to use the first method if a larger change is needed and the second technique for fine-tuning.

Now it's time to address what to do if the hole you are tuning is too high (sharp). Hopefully by making the flute tube and bore a bit long we have avoided this situation but it has happened to me. If you look really close at the smaller, darker flute on the cover you can see that the hole closest to the mouth-hole isn't quite right. This was one of my first flutes and I didn't know yet that the closer to the mouth-hole you get the more sensitive the adjustments must be.

Filling hole to lower its pitch

What I did, and I later found that others often do, is make up a small batch of epoxy mixed with some sanding-dust from the flute and fill the upper part of the sharp hole. It may take a few applications as the thickened epoxy might tend to shrink back a little as it cures. Once it has cured well (overnight, even with 5-minute epoxy, is best), try the note and reshape the hole to obtain the proper note and make the fix as unnoticeable as possible.

Work your way up the flute, one note at a time, from all holes covered to all holes open. Adjust the pitch as close as you can, using your pitch pipe, piano or tuner. We're not after super-accuracy here, just reasonably recognizable pitch. In fact, it is perfectly OK to forgo the tuning tools completely, and just tune each finger hole to a pitch that sounds good to you.

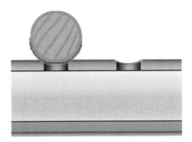

Softening the finger holes

The last thing you may want to do before putting a durable finish on your flute is to 'soften' the finger holes to make it easier and more comfortable to properly seal the holes. I wrap a piece of #320 sandpaper around a finger-tip sized dowel and carefully sand across the center of the hole. In the diagram above it looks like I'm sanding perpendicular to the length of the flute but what you really want to do is create very shallow ovals aimed in the direction your finger approaches each hole when holding the flute comfortably. Here is the way the flute is meant to be held from a player's point of view:

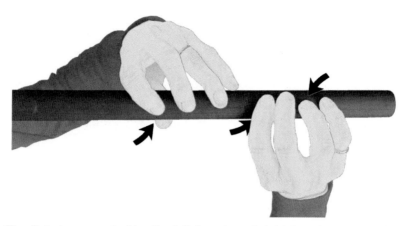

The flute is supported by the left thumb and right thumb and third finger

Hold the flute to your lips in approximately this position and one by one sand/soften each hole in the direction your finger lies over the hole. When you are done with this step go over the whole flute with #320 or #400 sandpaper and you will be ready for finishing.

12 – Finishing

It's time to put a nice, people-safe finish on the flute. I have used several different finishes over the years and am currently using a 50-50 blend of 100% pure tung oil and turpentine. You may have a favorite finish and really, anything that is food-safe and won't go rancid will work. What we're looking for is a finish that will penetrate the wood - hopefully all the way through, and cure. That leaves out mineral oil and unless you are very patient, raw linseed oil. My tung oil/turpentine mixture dries and cures in a couple of days. I like to wait to use the flute until it has no smell of turpentine.

I've made up a simple swab stick from 3/8" x 16" dowel by drilling a line of 1/8" holes about an inch long near one end and then cutting out the waste between the holes. A little strip of sandpaper run like a shoe-shine cloth through the opening will clean it up nicely. I slide a small piece of cloth through the slot, soak it in the oil mixture and run it up and down inside the bore, holding the tube vertically to ensure that the end beyond the mouth-hole gets its share.

After a few minutes you can alternately wipe the outside and swab the inside with clean cloth until no more finish comes off. Be sure to properly dispose of those oily rags safely! I throw mine in the wood-stove.

─────────────────────────────────────

If all has gone well, you should have in your hands a pretty nice little wooden flute. If this, your first try, didn't turn out as nice as you'd hoped you are at least a more experienced instrument maker and I suspect that you know just what to do to make your next one even better. I kept a few of my first flutes around for a while to help me perfect the process but eventually found that I had more fun if I approached each instrument as though it was my first – just going for it, using what I'd absorbed from prior projects. More flutes and more fun!

13 – Making a Case

My wife Sue is the case maker in our family. She sews up a simple tube from a piece of heavy, lined or quilted fabric 5 x 21-1/2" (about 6" longer than the flute). The top is hemmed and folded over the end of the flute. She sews on a piece of ribbon to secure that flap and keep the flute in its place. She has also made similar cases using deer skin and other soft leather.

Cloth & leather flute cases

Being a 'wood guy' I have made cherry boxes sized to fit the instruments. These usually have a simple leather hinge and clasp two leather-lined 'saddles' to secure the flutes inside.

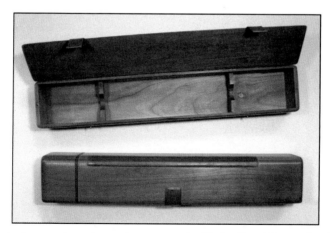

Flute boxes, top view: cherry wood with leather hinges & trim

14 – Playing Your First Tune

By now I'm sure that you have played more than just the notes needed to tune your new flute. So, what tune did you go for? If you are near my age you probably tried Yankee Doodle or some other tune of that nature that you might remember. Tunes that are traditionally played on a fife, whistle or flute are naturals for your flute. Actually, any tune or song that you can hear in your head and/or whistle would be good to start with. I've found that certain Christmas carols are so securely set in my brain that they are some of the easiest to play by ear. Whatever you have stored in your head - go for it!

If you read music then tunes that are in the keys of 'A' and 'D' will be a good place to start. Look for:

- Three sharps = Key of A   or

- Two sharps = Key of D

Tunes in A and D will be the easiest to play but you will soon find that tunes in the key of G are not too difficult using a technique called 'half-holing' where you sharpen or flatten a note by partially covering the finger hole above or below the usual note.

15 – Fingering Chart – What Notes to Play

I've made up this fingering chart to help you learn what finger-holes to cover to create a note on the musical scale. In the following section I've provided a half-dozen traditional songs and tunes. Use this chart to help get your fingers in the right place. Since it isn't convenient to flip back to this page while reading the sheet music, you can download and print the Fingering Chart from my web site:

www.manytracks.com/flutes/fingering-chart.pdf

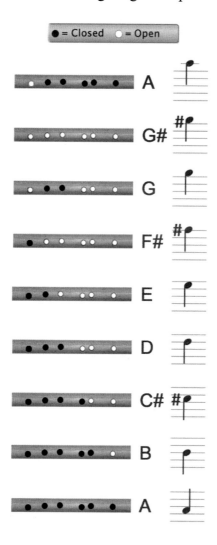

16 – Tunes

Here are a few traditional songs and tunes to get you started.

Amazing Grace
tune - New Britain

(w) John Newton 1779
put to "New Britain" tune 1846

Will the Circle Be Unbroken

Charles Gabriel (m), Ada Habershon (w), 1907

Aura Lee

W.W.Fosdick (w), George Poulton (m), 1861

Red River Valley

<1890, northern fur trade era song

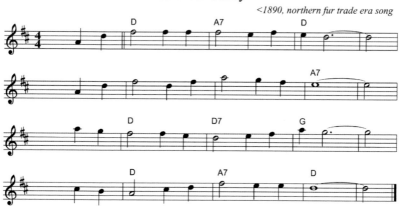

Ode to Joy
from Symphony No. 9 in D minor

Ludwig van Beethoven, 1824

Angelina Baker (Angeline the Baker)

orig. Stephen Foster 1850

###

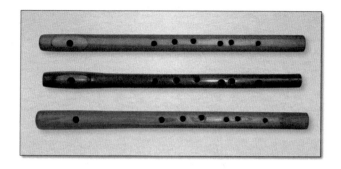

I hope that you have enjoyed reading this print version of my wooden flute making guide and that you have enjoyed making your own wood flute! Please feel free to contact me if you have any questions or comments on the building process. Your thoughts will be appreciated as I continue to work toward making it better.

If you do make a flute I'd love hear from you to see how it turned out. A photo of your flute would be nice too. If you enjoyed the book will you please take a moment to leave me a review at your favorite book retailer?

Thanks!

Steve

About the author

Steve Schmeck and his wife Sue Robishaw live on their backwoods homestead on 80 remote acres in Michigan's Upper Peninsula. They live in an 'underground', sod-roofed home that they built themselves, have a large organic garden that provides much of their food, and power their off-grid homestead with solar power.

Steve has been involved in art and woodworking since he was young, and it has permeated his life since. Majoring in Art in college, Steve emerged into his art career in the late 70's when he decided to realize his vision of living and sculpting in the Northwoods. He is now a nationally recognized bowl and spoon carver with both bowls and spoons in many private collections.

Other areas of interest are music (he is a fiddler), musical instrument restoration and repair, and recumbent bicycles (for years he rode a homebuilt, wood recumbent). Lately he has been celebrating his birthday by riding his age in miles on that day; last year, 70 miles. Next on his agenda is building a skin-on-frame dory for rowing along the shores of the northern Great Lakes.

Books published by ManyTracks

<u>PRINT BOOKS</u>

Make Your Own Treadle Lathe
by Steve Schmeck

Homesteading Adventures:
A Guide for Doers and Dreamers,
by Sue Robishaw, with Steve Schmeck

Frost Dancing: Tips from a Northern Gardener
by Sue Robishaw

The Last Lamp - a novel by Sue Robishaw

Rosita & Sian Search for a Great Work of Art
by Sue Robishaw

<u>EBOOKS</u>

Make Your Own Treadle Lathe
by Steve Schmeck

Homesteading Adventures:
A Guide for Doers and Dreamers,
by Sue Robishaw, with Steve Schmeck

Moving with the Music
a novella by Sue Robishaw

Frost Dancing: Tips form a Northern Gardener
by Sue Robishaw

<u>EBOOKS COMING SOON</u>

Growing Fruit the ManyTracks Way
by Sue Robishaw

Connect with Steve

On the web:

www.manytracks.com

Via Email:

steve@manytracks.com

Steve's Amazon Author Page:

http://www.amazon.com/Steve-Schmeck/e/B000APJWO0

<<<◇>>>

Made in the USA
Coppell, TX
29 August 2023

20955881R00031